NORTH DAKOTA

simply beautiful

photography by Chuck Haney

FARCOUNTRY
PRESS

Front cover: Hay bales
near Bottineau.

Back cover: Caprocks in
Little Missouri National
Grassland.

Title page: Grain bins,
Williston.

Right: On Lake
Sakakawea.

ISBN 1-56037-192-7
© 2001 Farcountry Press
Photographs © by Chuck
Haney unless otherwise
indicated

For more information on our
books write:
Farcountry Press,
P.O. Box 5630, Helena, MT
59604 or call: (800) 654-1105 or
visit:www.montanamagazine.com
Created, produced, and designed
in the United States.
Printed in Korea.

Foreword

I've immensely enjoyed the diversity of the land in North Dakota. The vast prairie grasslands that North Dakota is known for are book-ended by the fertile black soil of the Red River Valley in the east and the amazing badlands in the west. In between, teeming pothole wetlands fill with seasonal migratory birds. With monikers like Hoople, Gackle and Bowbells, small towns lace the farm fields, where grain elevators and water towers compete as landmarks. The northern strip of land that borders the Canadian provinces of Saskatchewan and Manitoba is quite different from the rest of the state. It's amazing what a few hundred feet of elevation gain can do. Myriad small lakes support healthy populations of moose, while aspen and birch forests dot the rolling landscape and turn golden in the fall chill. My favorite North Dakota terrain is the western badlands. I have ridden my mountain bike, hiked, and ridden a horse into the heart of the backcountry. Coming around the bend of the Maah Daah Hey Trail among towering sandstone monuments to a remote valley brimming with wildflowers, or camping along the Little Missouri River under the shade of a stately cottonwood grove, is to feel wonderfully alive!

I've met a lifetime's worth of friendly and wonderful people throughout the state. One morning at sunrise, along the Viking Scenic highway near Fort Ransom, I was standing on an aluminum ladder at the edge of a field filled with tall, brightly blooming sunflowers. Something you see every day, right? An older farmer gentleman was cruising along the lonely gravel road inspecting his crops when he spied me perched among his sunflower tops. Of course, he pulled over to inquire as to my intentions (maybe my sanity, too). We struck up a friendly conversation; after all, I'm an old farmboy who still speaks the lingo. Finally, the farmer asked me, "What's your last name?" "Haney," I replied. "Haney! that's not Norwegian! What good are ya!" We laughed. Bigshot photographer done in by Scandinavian humor.

North Dakota is forever a land of magical moments for me. I had hiked several miles into a remote valley full of petrified wood stumps in the wilderness area of Theodore Roosevelt National Park's south unit. I photographed these amazing pedestals of ancient sequoia tree stumps until the day's last light dipped below the grassy table to the west. Hiking out, I met five bison bulls grazing near the trail. I gingerly and very respectfully made my way among these magnificent creatures, my adrenalin pumping. After I had passed by, I turned around to witness the full moon rising behind the buffalo. Here, alone with the buffalo on an endless grassy plain and a full moonrise was primal America. Where's the photo of this? you may ask. Some "photos" are best kept upstairs, vivid and well preserved by memory. Besides, I'm not that crazy! I didn't tempt fate that dusky evening, since an angry buffalo can outrun an Olympic sprinter. I just walked away slowly, soaking the wonder of it all in.

North Dakota can cast a spell. I was driving west on Highway 200 just east of Hazen at dusk feeling the sense of freedom that such a empty stretch of road can bring (think *Easy Rider)*. In the waning light, I saw that here was the spot where the Midwest turns into the American West. An uncanny feeling crept over me as I saw the landscape change from grassy prairie to rolling and broken badlands. North Dakota had done it again.

North Dakota ranks first in the United States in sunflower production, supplying more than half the nation's sunflower seeds.

Above: Wild-turkey hens interrupted during their morning chat.

Right: The Little Missouri River flows north through Theodore Roosevelt National Park, South Unit.

Above: The nearly 60,000 acres of the J. Clark Salyer National Wildlife Refuge, near Minot, can see half a million waterfowl as autumn draws on.

Facing page: Tipi poles rise above shortgrass prairie near the Montana border.

Above: Prairie coneflower.

Left: Scoria, or lava, formations in Little Missouri National Grasslands, McKenzie County.

Rugged wild horses roam free on Theodore National Park, South Unit (above), while the Little Missouri River sculpts sandbars on the North Unit (facing page).

Above: Nineteenth-century homesteaders built hundreds of country churches across North Dakota.

Left: Sweet spring is here!

Above: The Yellowstone River flows into the Missouri right at the
North Dakota–Montana border.

Facing page: Gambrel roof and red-oxide paint: an American classic.

Above: This movie palace has been serving Fargo residents since it opened with silent films and vaudeville acts in 1926.

Right: Stormy sunset over the Little Muddy River near Williston.

Left: Yellow-headed blackbirds can be found in Sheyenne National Grasslands in Richland County.

Below: The Petrified Forest of Theodore Roosevelt National Park, South Unit.

Facing page: At Knife River Indian Villages National Historic Site near Stanton, visitors learn of life in the late 1700s and early 1800s among the Mandan Indians, who lived in substantial earth lodges like this one.

Above: Whichever direction you're going, you're halfway there, so sit for a spell.

Left: Alfalfa a-growing near Grassy Butte.

Above: In the International Peace Garden along the North Dakota–Manitoba border, a tribute to U.S.–Canada relations.

Right: Fiery sky over Fort Stevenson State Park.

Refreshed by a passing rainstorm, Painted Canyon in Theodore Roosevelt National Park, South Unit.

Above: Several 7th Cavalry privates carved their names on Initial Rock, now in Little Missouri Grasslands, en route from Fort Abraham Lincoln (near Mandan) to attack Sioux and Cheyenne in June 1876. Company H rode into battle at the Little Bighorn under Captain Benteen, not Lt. Col. Custer, and Williams survived.

Right: A muskrat grooms itself at home, Sheyenne National Grasslands.

Facing page: Once upon a time a leaf fell into some mud, and—geological ages later—was hidden in the center of a "cannonball concretion" in Theodore Roosevelt National Park, North Unit.

Oliver County hay bales.

Above: A great blue heron scouts for a snack near Abercrombie.

Facing page: Cold sky above, fresh snow below—near Scoria
Point in Theodore Roosevelt National Park, South Unit.

Above: Nearly-ripe sunflower crop on a Langdon farm.

Facing page: White Butte, the state's highest point at 3,506 feet, rises above Bowman-area badlands.

Aspens border a Rolette County field.

Commonly called "antelope," the pronghorn was first scientifically described as
"the goat of this country" by the Lewis and Clark Expedition.

Above: North Dakota's two oldest standing buildings built by a Euro-American are the restored home and trading post of Antoine Gingras, now a state historic site near Walhalla.

Facing page: Red scoria road near Belfield.

Above: Mountain bikers ford the Little Missouri River to follow the Maah Daah Hey Trail.

Facing page: Chimney-spire and caprock formations of Little Missouri National Grassland.

Visitors to Fort Union Trading Post National Historic Site, near Williston, see reconstructed palisades and buildings as they would have appeared in the early 1850s, when the fort's managers received goods from St. Louis to trade for furs.

41

Above: Grain truck near Enderlin.

Facing page: De Mores State Historic Site, outside Medora, holds the 26-room "chateau" built by the town's founder, a French marquis, on his cattle ranch.

Glowing sunflowers.

The American bison once filled these prairies
in the tens of thousands.

Near Devils Lake, Sully's Hill National Game Preserve supports a green ash forest as part of its environmental training facilities.

Sandstone layers lit afire by sunset, Theodore Roosevelt
National Park, South Unit.

Above: Autumn mosaic in Lake Metigoshe State Park, which offers year-round recreation opportunities north of Bottineau.

Facing page: Islands in Lake Sakakawea, the Missouri River backed up by Garrison Dam, once were prairie hilltops.

Above: Every night from mid-June through Labor Day, Burning Hills Amphitheater fills with the Medora Musical, which tells stories from Dakota Territory history and about characters including Theodore Roosevelt, who briefly ranched nearby in his younger days.

Left: A farmer's hours during wheat harvest are many and long.

Mule deer bucks, alert at dawn.

Badlands above the Little Missouri River.

Above: Pasqueflowers are a harbinger of summer.

Left: A study in badlands erosion.

Above: Plains Indian tipis, formerly made of animal hides, were pulled from campsite to campsite by dogs before the horse arrived on the northern Great Plains.

Facing page: North Dakota supplies three fourths of the United States' canola oil, from fields like these that bloom in gold.

Cottonwood trees on the bank and sandbars in the water: a typical Missouri River scene.

Historic saltbox-style barn along the Viking Scenic Highway.

Twilight's brush heightens badlands'
eerie appearance.

Right: Morning coffee must be brewing on this Amtrak passenger train as it zips through Devils Lake. Once, multiple Great Northern Railway trains stopped here each day.

Below: Downtown Devil's Lake.

Facing page: Bison skull on McKenzie County shortgrass prairie.

Right: The "world's largest bison statue," at Jamestown's Frontier Village museum, stands three stories high and weighs sixty tons.

Below: In Washburn's Fort Mandan Park (about ten miles from the original's location) stands this replica of the self-built fort where nearly forty whites—men of the Lewis and Clark Expedition—spent the winter of 1804-1805.

Facing page: The story of badlands is one of erosion, as water scours relatively soft rock.

Above: Cattle on the Oster Ranch in Mercer County,
part of the nearly 2 million beef cattle raised annually on
14,000 North Dakota ranches. TOM BEAN PHOTO

Right: A frigid winter night approaches St. Paul Church
in Mercer County. TOM BEAN PHOTO

Wheat in shocks at Sunne Demonstration Farm, a part of Fort Ransom State
Park that was settled in 1884 and now shows methods the homesteaders used.

Left: Wild turkeys flourish in North Dakota.

Below: A gentle nuzzle despite those horns.

Above: International Order of Odd Fellows lodge building in downtown Devils Lake dates from 1885, when lodge rooms were upstairs and the ground floor was leased to businesses.

Facing page: In the 1870s, railroads began to take North Dakota crops to market—and to bring in more homesteaders to raise and ship more crops.

Right: When Lewis and Clark first saw prairie dogs, they called them "barking squirrels."

Below: Before Norwegian immigrant Theodore Slattum became one of Ransom County's major landowners, he and his wife and seven children lived in this cabin.

In springtime, the Little Missouri River beckons canoeists.

The Red River, swollen with spring runoff, creeps up the banks.

A historic Lutheran Church, at home amid farm fields.

Left: Appropriately named foxtail barley.

Below: Loading harvested soybeans into a truck.

Badlands at nightfall.

Above: This unusual round barn combination, at Dunseith, also served as a square-dance hall.

Facing page: As far as the camera can see, from White Butte.

Right: Burr oak leaves add to autumn brilliance.

Below: Lewis and Clark Interpretive Center, Washburn, exhibits reproduction and period gear and clothing used by the expedition as it passed through here in 1805 and 1806.

Facing page: Rough shoreline along Lake Sakakawea.

Above: Standard-design frontier army officer quarters, this building was home to Lt. Col. and Mrs.
George A. Custer at Fort Abraham Lincoln, his last post and today a state park.

Facing page: Autumn is winding down.

Knife River crossing.

A misty sunrise in the Turtle Mountains.

Above: Nearly time to harvest the field corn.

Right: Burning off the morning fog.

Facing page: Native grasses carpet the land right up to intriguing rock formations.

Minot Air Force Base, Minot State University—and annual events like the Norsk Høstfest and North Dakota State Fair—enliven the north-central city of 35,000.

Old but still useful in the Sheyenne River Valley.

Above: Grain elevators are the anchor for many a town's business district, as here at Walhalla, population about 1200.

Facing page: Find "Waldo the Bison."

Above: Purple coneflower.

Left: Badlands shapes in McKenzie County.

Above: Elk cows and calves debate what to do about that man with the black box.

Facing page: Once a trail to a Mandan village, now a farm track in Knife River country.

Right: This cottontail rabbit "knows" she's invisible as long as she stays perfectly still.

Below: Day's end during soybean harvest.

Facing page: Another beautiful day dawns in western North Dakota.

Above: Wild prairie rose is North Dakota's state flower.

Left: Lush growth near Lone Butte.

Left: North Dakota is within the breeding range of the Canada goose.

Below: Minot's Scandinavian Heritage Park honors the ethnic backgrounds of North Dakotans from Denmark, Finland, Iceland, Norway and Sweden.

Four Bears Bridge crosses Lake Sakakawea on Fort Berthold Reservation, home to the Three Affiliated Tribes (Arikara, Hidatsa, and Mandan).

A bright prairie moon over Mercer County.

Above: Busy at work on marsh marigolds at Mirror Pool Wildlife
Management Area.

Right: Double beauty over the badlands.

Right: Cautiously, a bull moose assesses his surroundings.

Below: Swans out for a paddle below the watchful eye of a bald eagle.

Facing page: A prairie sentinel at Hazen.

Right: Just days old, a bison calf explores its world.

Below: The next corn crops goes into fertile Red River Valley soil.

Facing page: Downhill on a single track—one way to enjoy the badlands.

Warm welcome awaits at Lake Metigoshe State Park.

Sunrise highlights the foxtail barley beside Lake Sakakawea.

On the Satrom farm near Colgate, combines harvest wheat that will add to North Dakota's $500 million worth of wheat for the year. TOM BEAN PHOTO

North Dakota Scenic Byway welcomes drivers with aspen splendor at Pembina Gorge.

Gackle, population 450, is a service center for Logan County.

Above: Morning dew bejewels the Turtle Mountains.

Left: The Yellowstone—longest free-flowing river in the continental U.S.—peacefully meets the Mighty Mo.

At Fort Abercrombie State Park, the fort's original guardhouse (dating from 1858) and reconstructed blockhouse and stockade show one of the first federal posts in future North Dakota, built to protect Red River traffic.

A new day creeps into the Turtle Mountains.

Following page: Autumn glory in the Pembina River Gorge.